BACK TO SCHOOL VOCABULARY

Carefully look at each box. Unscramble the word and write it below.

uhps ipn

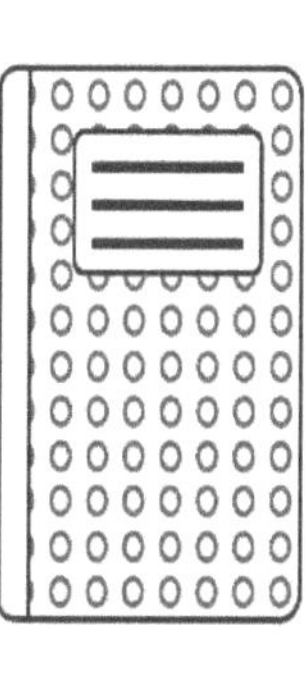

bonoteok

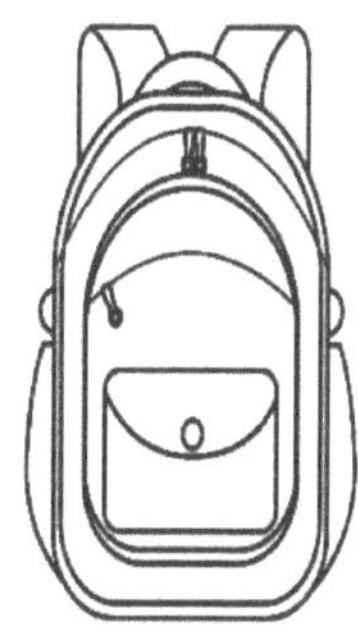

abg

legu

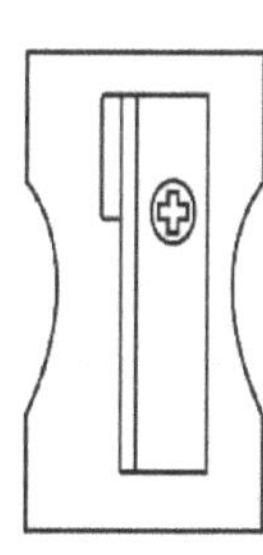

nerrpesha

obko

BACK TO SCHOOL VOCABULARY

Carefully look at each box. Unscramble the
word and write it below.

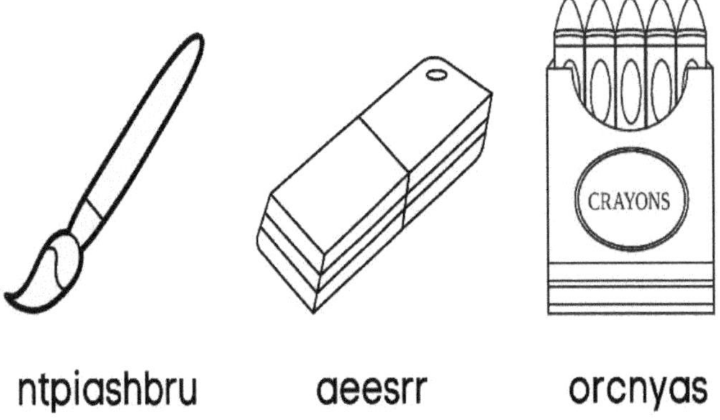

ntpiashbru   aeesrr   orcnyas

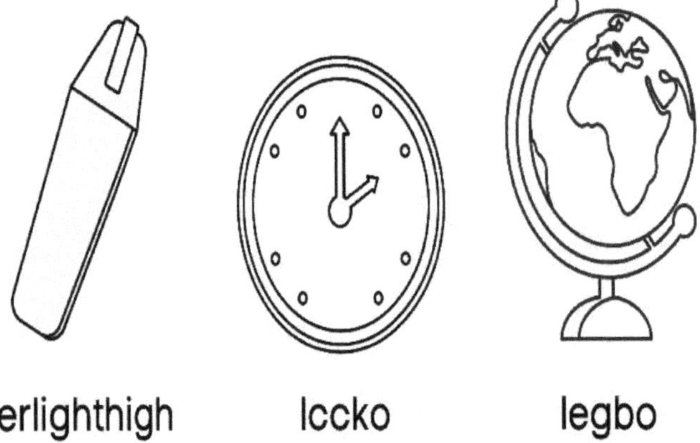

erlighthigh   lccko   legbo

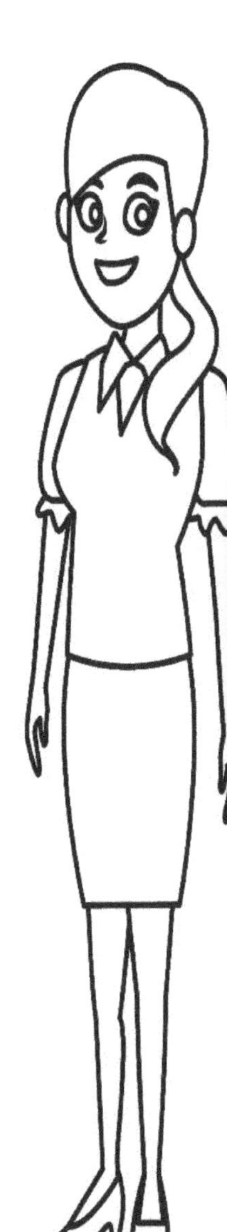

Walking to School is fun

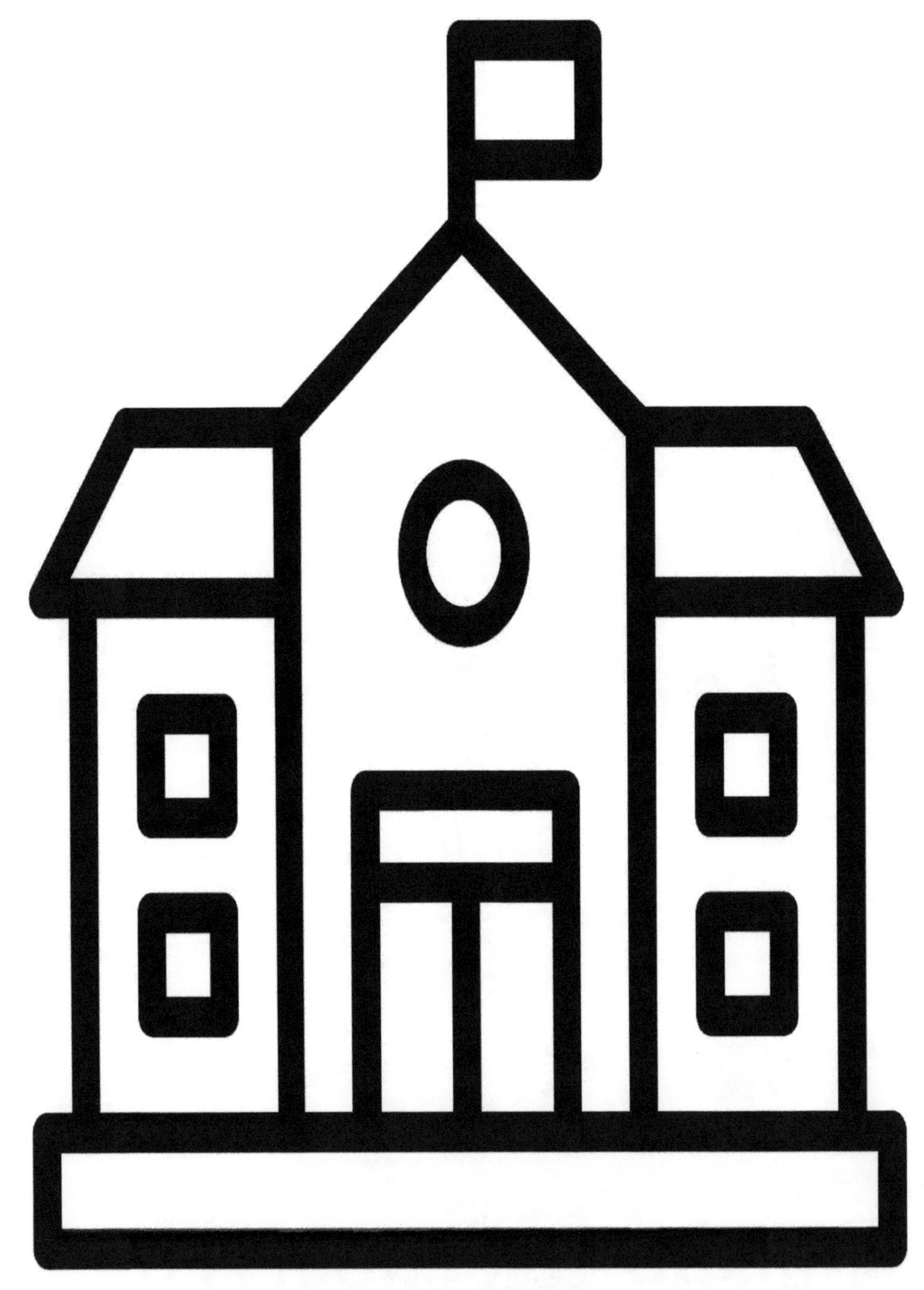

The School house

Learning is fun

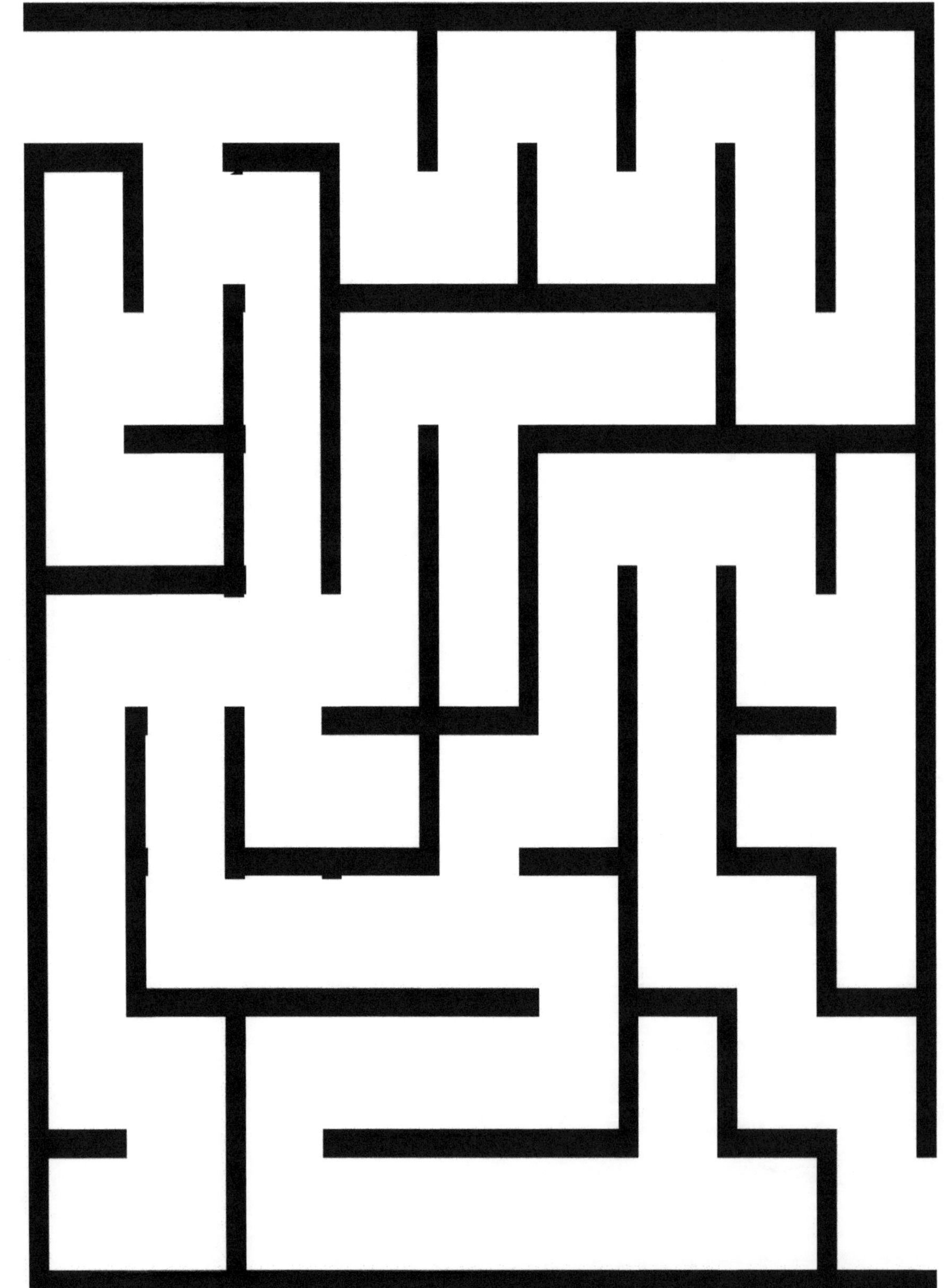

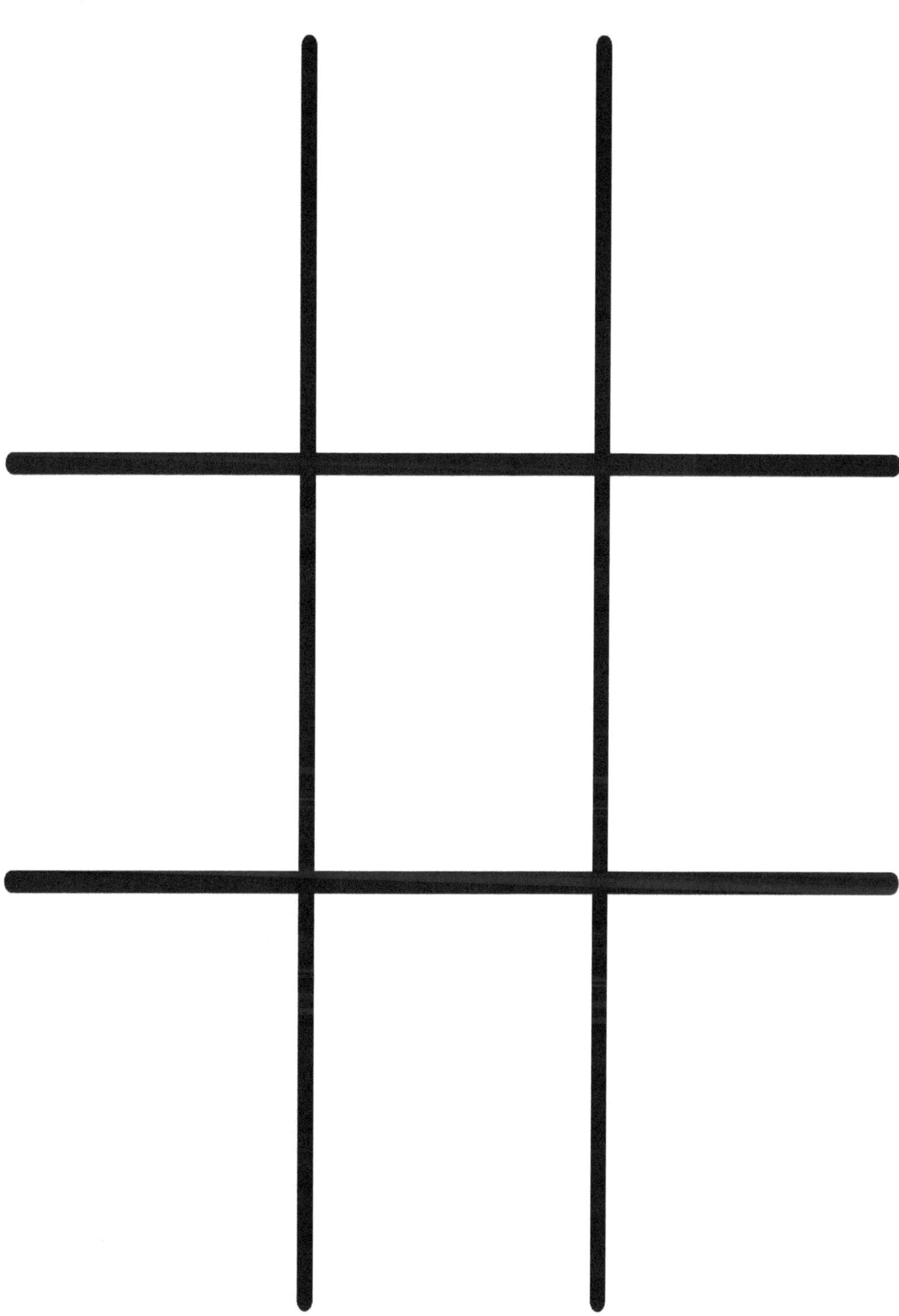

I Love to read

2+2
Math is Cool

School Supplies

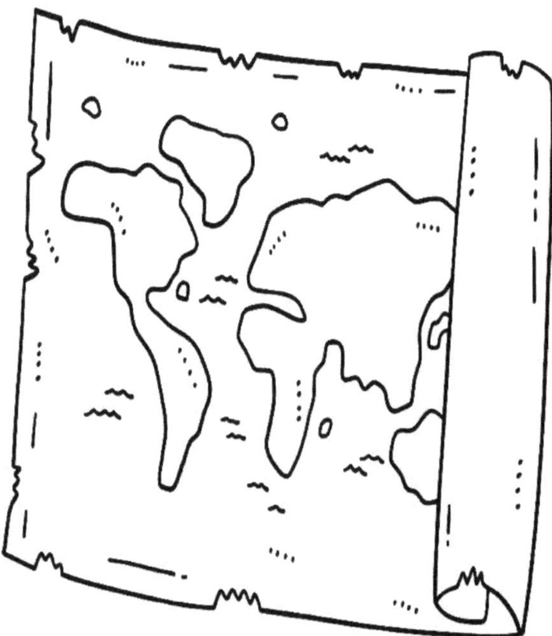

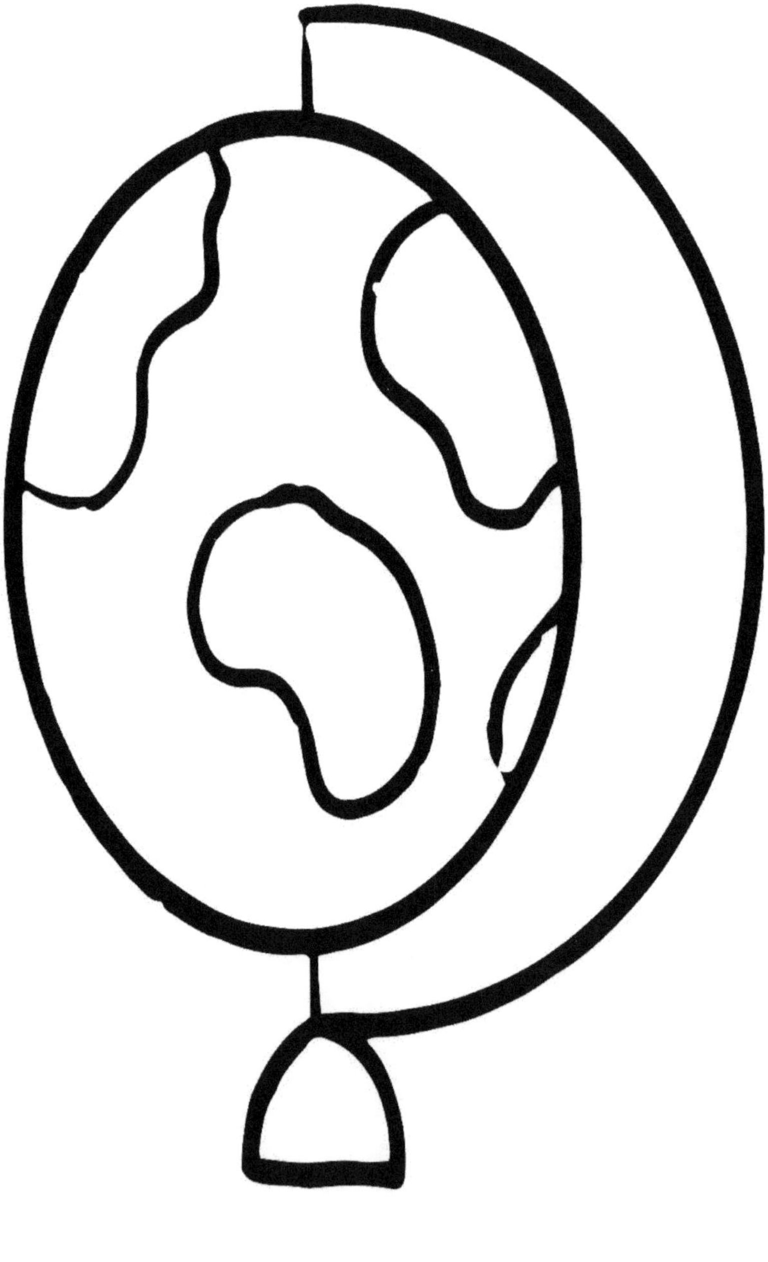

I learn about
the world

Learning is Bright

I love building things

I use the internet to Learn

Excersice is fun

I love making friends

I love learning

I learn about the weather

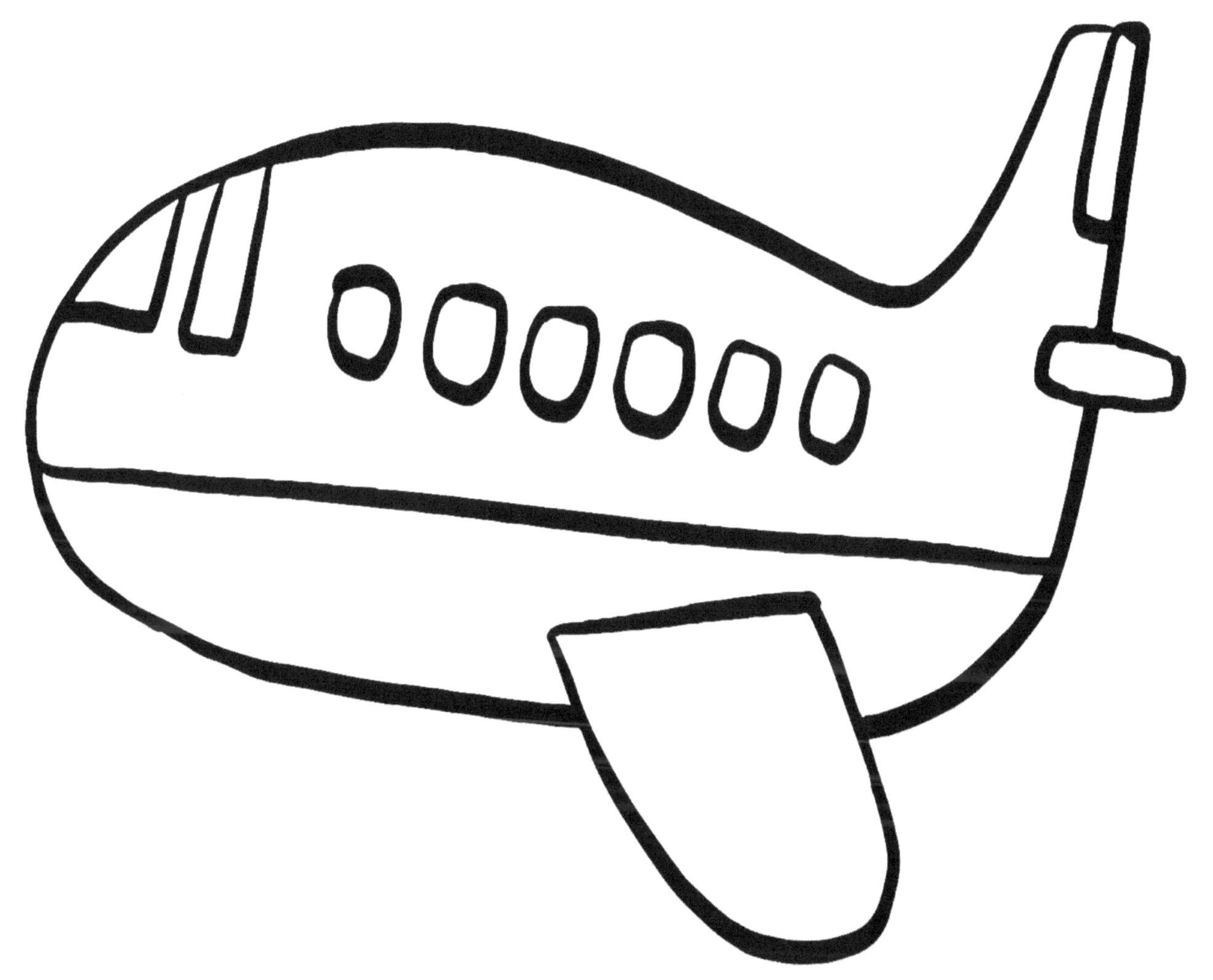

I learned about transportation

I learn to play music

Match the Sentence

Sentence		
This is a dog.		
The boy reads.		
A baby crawls.		
I see a lion.		
This is a bag.		
These are pens.		

We love to learn

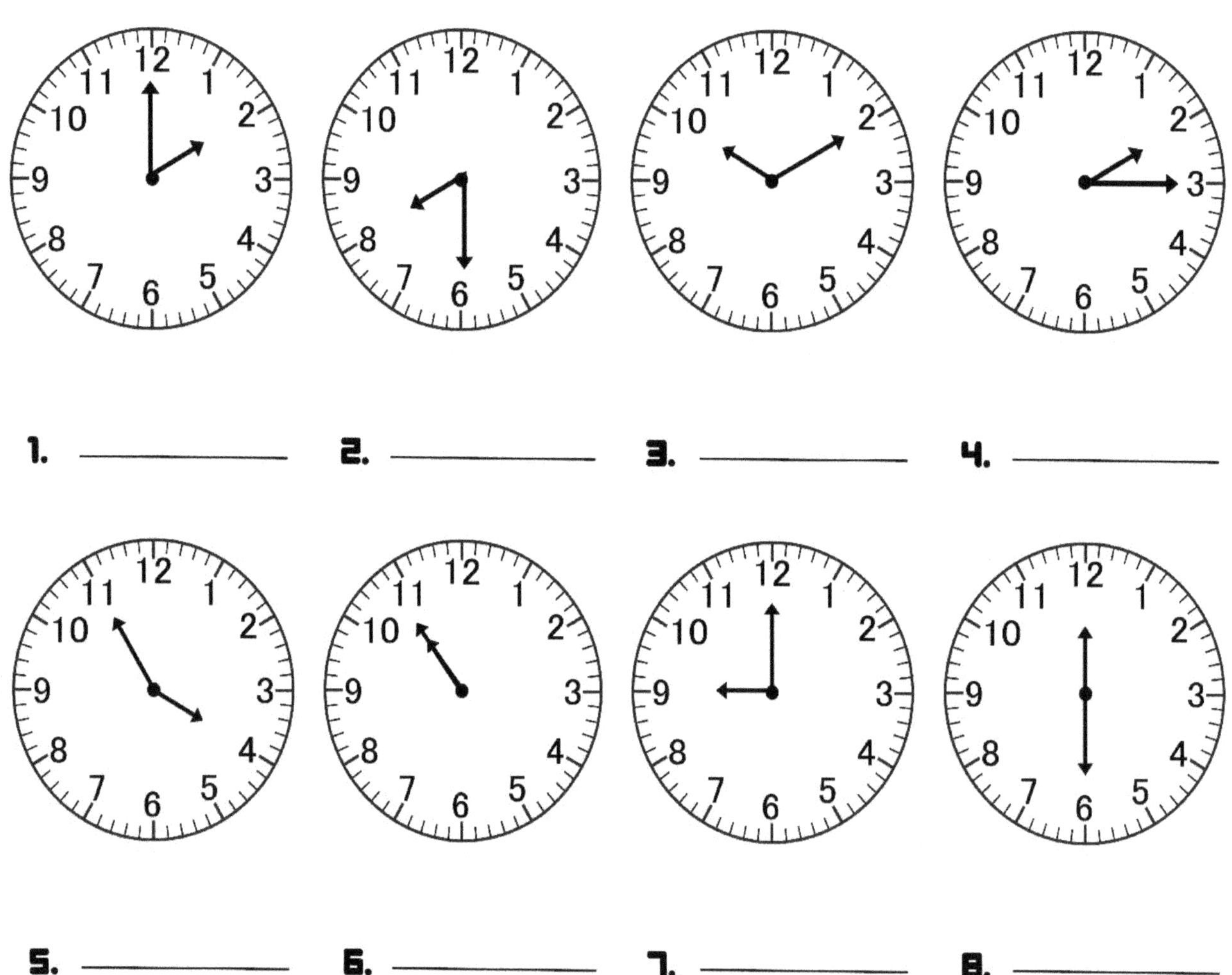

1. _______________   2. _______________   3. _______________   4. _______________

5. _______________   6. _______________   7. _______________   8. _______________

Write the times shown on the clocks.